The Vagabond Scholar

The Vagabond Scholar

Poems of My Life and Thought in Several European Lands

William Franke

CASCADE *Books* • Eugene, Oregon

THE VAGABOND SCHOLAR
Poems of My Life and Thought in Several European Lands

Cascade Books
An Imprint of Wipf and Stock Publishers
199 W. 8th Ave., Suite 3
Eugene, OR 97401

www.wipfandstock.com

PAPERBACK ISBN: 979-8-3852-6476-6
HARDCOVER ISBN: 979-8-3852-6477-3
EBOOK ISBN: 979-8-3852-6478-0

Cataloguing-in-Publication data:

Names: Franke, William [author].

Title: The vagabond scholar : poems of my life and thought in several European lands / William Franke.

Description: Eugene, OR: Cascade Books, 2026.

Identifiers: ISBN 979-8-3852-6476-6 (paperback) | ISBN 979-8-3852-6477-3 (hardcover) | ISBN 979-8-3852-6478-0 (ebook)

Subjects: LCSH: American poetry—20th century. | Travel—Poetry. | Poetry of places. | Poetry.

Classification: PR605.S44 F73 2026 (paperback) | PR605.S44 (ebook)

VERSION NUMBER 04/09/26

Cover Image. *Arthur Rimbaud en marche* by CharlÉlie Couture, Musée de la Chartreuse, Douai (France). By kind permission of the Museum.

CONTENTS

ILLUSTRATIONS

Appendix: Supplementary Photo Album

Figure 1. *Arthur Rimbaud en marche* by CharlÉlie Couture, Musée de la Chartreuse, Douai (France). By kind permission of the Museum.

Preface

THESE POEMS WERE WRITTEN in the 1980s after I had completed my MA degree in philosophy and theology at Oxford University. In May 1980, I "went down" from Oxford, as one says, and embarked on the notorious "grand tour" of Europe in the tradition of British aristocrats from the seventeenth to the nineteenth centuries. The "tour" often lasted for several years, as it did in my case. At the time, however, I was not consciously following this pattern but only taking up an invitation from some generous Italians, who were attending courses for teaching English and happened to be lodged in the same "digs" as a theology classmate and bosom companion of mine. We often shared common meals together, and they invited me to come and live with them in Turin. This allowed me to learn Italian by total immersion, like a child.

The poems are situated largely in Italy and France, as well as in England. Thanks to networks of connections among friends in the exceptionally hospitable peninsula stretching from Piedmont to Sicily, together with a providential dose of serendipity, I sojourned as a house guest in Florence, Rome, Naples, Palermo, and elsewhere. I also continued to traverse France, as I hitchhiked between Italy and Great Britain. During this period, I worked intermittently in London, in the social sector and in theatre, and was able at several stages to serve in Paris as an artistic tour guide for Italians at the cathedral Notre Dame de Paris.

I returned to the US in 1984, concluding this season as an itinerant poet and taking up jobs, mostly teaching in private schools, before entering upon a doctoral program in Comparative Literature, first at UC Berkeley and finally at Stanford (PhD, 1991).

From that point on, I was overwhelmingly occupied with critical and philosophical writing in an academic vein. The verses that I, nevertheless, continued to generate are collected in a companion volume titled *The Thoughtful Muse: Autobiography in Occasional Verse* (Cascade Books, 2026). Its more stripped-down, telegraphic style aims to register moments of life and thought immediately rather than to produce artistically elaborated compositions. That style contrasts with the volume in hand distinguished by its youthful inspirations and lyrical transports in a more musical mode and aesthetically measured manner. The poems presented here are the work of the vagabond in Europe of the 1980s, who lived and breathed poetry like his alter ego a century earlier, the iconic French vagabond poet Arthur Rimbaud (1854–91).

Of course, further back in medieval times, more distant antecedents traversed the same territory in the shapes of the wandering scholars or "goliards" of the eleventh and twelfth centuries, some of whose voices resound in the *Carmena Burana* (Carl Orff, 1937). Troubadours, too, migrated from court to court, which they graced with inspired pieces of universal Song. Such avatars represent social classes widely diverse from the touring aristocrats, but all these precedents capture aspects of my peregrinations and their exploratory spirit of wonderstruck wandering. English Romantic poets Shelley, Byron, and Keats also crossed this terrain in variously self-exilic rovings that resonate here as well.

My collection begins from the end of the adventure, with its first poem, "Paranoia: Beyond the Pearly Harbor," written shortly after my return to the United States, marking the closure of this era of not always carefree *vagabondaggio*.

ACKNOWLEDGMENTS

A few of these poems were published previously in magazines or journals noted as follows:

"Dance of the Shirts," *The Writer*, November 1984

"Letter to a Friend," "March," *SEAMS: The Cultural Art Journal*, Volume 2, No. 1, Fall 1985

"Free Riding I–IV," *SEAMS: The Cultural Arts Journal*, Volume 2, No. 2, Winter–Spring 1986

"Glimpses I–IV," *SEAMS: The Cultural Arts Journal*, Volume 2, No. 3, Summer–Fall 1986

"Limbo," "Faring Well in Arms," "Lightspot," *SEAMS: The Cultural Arts Journal*, Volume 2, No. 4, Winter–Spring 1987

"Original Lyric," "Outsight," *BERKELEY POETS 1987* (Rosenberg Prize)

The artworks reproduced are in the public domain. Pictures of public monuments have been garnered from the internet from sources that are in the public domain or freely available for further use on condition of acknowledgement of their sources. They are generally available through Wikimedia Commons and under the Creative Commons Agreement.

The vagabond scholar had no camera and took no pictures. He recorded sights only through poetic description, which registers personal impressions rather than the outward public appearance of places. Nevertheless, the photographic images might help others who did not participate in the experiences described to imagine their contexts and understand them.

There are innumerable individuals to whom I am forever indebted for making my migrations possible and for sharing in my adventures and discoveries. I can expressly name and thank only a fraction among the most principal and prominent: Ornella Cazzullo, Marina Rista, Gian Ferrero, Giovanni Laino, Lina, Maria, Angelo, Guido, and Silvia Baldi, Maria Teresa Porta, Annarita and Cesare Diegoli, Cinzia Marocchino, Giancarlo, Roberto Zannone, Adrianna Coda, Dave Kirkwood, Graham Shaw, Eileen and Tony Jones. I owe especially the Italian people as a whole my undying gratitude for their warm embrace and sympathetic fostering of an expatriate scholar and his unconventional quest. They accepted and welcomed me and made me feel myself a naturalized Italian by adoption and predilection.

Liminal

PARANOIA: BEYOND THE PEARLY HARBOR

On the day when the skies rained
And home security burst in a shower of Japanese fireworks
Startling me from unquiet sleep
To my senses screaming
Of what was wrong
And I saw the world
And I saw
Suburbanites cruising in bombers
Sitting placidly yet implacable over their engines
Driving at me
To the drone of easy listening drowning out cries from far away
From the jungles of Guatemala
From the shores of the Philippines
From the embattled peoples of the Levant rising up
In acrid crimson waves
From seared off flesh of yellow limbs left rotting in rice patties
And from Hiroshima gibbering
Flitting graveless across the scene.
Suddenly their voices were piercing and plainly intelligible to me
Who hapless and hurting
And without a job
My education by now being forfeit to my non-conformity

Come crashing home out of clouds overseas
Was pressed by the pavements
My old paths
Closing round to reduce me from liberty
To body without mind or sex
Lumping me in at the base to be stepped on
By those positioned in a higher place.
And the beautiful bases of luxury I had never wanted but liked to see
Turned sinister now every feature
Projecting power
Against the likes of me
Their loves deployed in ingenious expensiveness
Fields of private rights
And weapons of fun
The whole prestigious apparatus elaborating their implicit intents
Of serried defense
Against aching guts of man in the guttered streets
Whose spirits shrink
And against those souls
Whose daily bread is defeat and whose shattered hearts
Beat wildly up against heaven
Perpetually excluded
From every club
Too crushed to care for themselves in their desperateness caring
Anyway
With whom I closed ranks
For the first time knowing that I had not yet been
And could not be away.

Continental (Italy and France)

ATMOSFERA VENEZIANA

Resplendent Venice, by the sea,
civilization's richest key
is struck in you. Like a vast open palace
of sculptured marble and intricate glass
you're a realm self-contained
and containing an ocean,
an artwork whose internal order gives motion
to nature attuned
to a human vision and harmony.
Here one walks not on earth but on architecture
and one breathes not plain air but an atmosphere
of such vibrant color and tone as flow
from the brushes of Titian and Tintoretto.
The ocean flows in each thoroughfare
And the sea breeze breathes on the wine-ripe air,
for Venice is swathed in an atmosphere
of mingled sea and sun and air.
By material limits unconfined
These three elements refined
her miracles compose.
And sustaining all that to sense shows,
her substance is but art,

which fills the space in every part.
O I know your day of splendor's past,
that you are crumbling frighteningly fast.
No more do ceremonious Doges ride,
trimmed in richest gala pride,
on the Grand Canal in the gondola of state
and draw to every balcony all that is ornate.
Now tourists milling round all ways
Clog damp and smelly callés,
Where the cats leap over the pigeon shit
And the street sweeps try to clean up a bit.
Yet though you are now but a memory,
a dream of the past afloat the sea,
as long as to the eye you bring
of your glory yet a glimmering
your image will still enamor me.

Figure 2. Venice, Rialto Bridge

BY THE ROMAN THEATRE, FIESOLE

Time is ticking in the bricks of these old peasant houses
And in the barreled slates upon their roofs:
Almost audibly, what time the brisk wind shakes
In leaves of trees
And by an alchemy of shade and light
Turns the stony surfaces to waves,
Like a mirage which on the instant will evaporate.
And in the flickering shimmer, burning forms and figures seem discernible,
Of upraised arms with swords and horses pawing furiously the air:
Of straining shoulders bruised and cut by harnesses of chains:
The tumultuous images of all ages,
Of tearing limbs and murderous rages,
All struggling in vain against the crisis which consumes them,
Like beating on brick walls.
But now, and just as suddenly as they arose, the flames subside,
And leave the houses sitting in the stillness of their yellow hue,
So soft and fine, in intimacy with the sun,
Which lays the stony masses back into their summer sleep,
As imperturbable again as all those ancient ruins lying by.

Figure 3. Roman Amphitheater at Fiesole (Florence, Italy)

POLITEAMA GARIBALDI, PALERMO

Many ancient and imperial themes may still be seen
in certain quarters of the city. Rounding a street corner
into view a Roman rotunda, massive, theatrical whirls.
Its Corinthian sculptured columns drum round murals
Of Pompeian color, ores and resins of the earth—
sun-drenched, like those Mediterranean tribes
who raised the wild satyr dance on the foam sea's edge.
Monumental stands their memory, tiered in double orders,
perfect form in marble balanced mathematically.
Yet the swirling drapery of the gesturing statuary leaning out
from niches and careening over the architrave,
the interlocking frenzy of the figures in the portal frieze,
and the sensuous distortion of the frescoes, don't all tell
the temper of a civilization riding waves and horses,
chafed and reining hard and tilting headlong in the spray?
This old spiritual agitation, this excitement of the sun,
is culture's perennial form, the order even of our day.
Here I am at home walking over Europe's furthest strand
and dare hope for our antics an historical existence.

Figure 4. Politeama Garibaldi, Palermo

NOSTALGIA PROVOKED BY A PORTRAIT OF CATERINA SFORZA BY LORENZO DI CREDI

Such portraiture is almost tastable
And smells like wine at noon,
Its oily vapors dancing out
In colored particles
Of sun or sea or flesh.
I am charmed and then transported
By the quiet physiognomy,
Which shows in loggia shadows,
Where calm composure coolly stares,
Backed by country blazed in southern sun.
For looking is like touching you,
Your olive-texture skin.
And the unsmiling, pleasant gaze
Of humanized antiquity
Is like the unfrivolous pleasure in
Your eyes brimful of Italian sky.
Your skin, its glow, your attitude
And the smell of wine at noon
Are the classics of all ages:
In them are body presence
And serenity of sea or sky.

Figure 5. *Portrait of Caterina Sforza* (1462–1509). Lorenzo di Credi, 1485–90. Pinacoteca Civica of the Musei San Domenico, Forlì, Italy

CONFESSION OF A MUSEUM-GOER IN ITALY

"I've seen much finer women ripe and real
Than all this nonsense of their stone ideal."

—Lord Byron

What are these consummately crafted shapes
I keep noticing
Of stockinged calves and neat-trimmed hips
And bosoms smartly corseted?
What rare art is embodied in these common forms of loveliness
Which no matter where I dwell
Is ever freshly springing up
To catch my breath and make my bosom swell?

ANOTHER CONFESSION: BY A WEARY PHILOSOPHER

Teach me gentleness and grace
Such as light upon that face
Wherein your own sweet self you show
Raffaello Sanzio.
Had I such beauty rare,
So perfect, fine and debonair,
Why should I need to be wise?
What would lack of Paradise?

THE STUDIO

The sun lies slant on the windowsill
As the picture leans against the wall,
Both unfinished.
Fingers ticking round the dial
Enamel in prismatic style
Pastel house and hill.
The afternoon lies down intense
Amidst the natural monuments,
Iridescent.
Like music from a harp that's played,
The one that Leonardo made,
Blooms the day.

OBSEQUIES, TURIN, FEBRUARY 9, 1983

Holy, holy, holy lord
God of the universe
to you we pray,
who else can we turn to now
very life is plucked away?
Immortality like music
Trembling within organ pipes
Is felt in fleeing,
descanted by
the cardinal robed in centuries,
the presidential presence in his tears.
Lord, God of the universe,
only when you take away
the nothing of our infinity
realize we the solemness
and weight of life with us.

STEEPLE BELL, PIEDMONT

Ringing, ringing, ringing
It rings, slowly expanding
Inundating the town
Steeped in ceremonies
Weathers and centuries
All in the air
All simultaneously there
In the ringing
Which rings from the center
And core of the earth
Of the metal resounding
Of everything, everyone
Compacted in
The vibration.

VIVALDI

Flutes fluttering in the belly
Mandolin strings plucked within me:
O Vivaldi, Vivaldi!
For a moment full of the universe
Of elegant young men and Venice
And the distilled sweetness of a century of genius
I was no longer man but only music:
Trilling, thrilling musical delight was all my being.

GABRIELLI

Horns heaving
Chords warmed
In the heart's pride
Of stately Venice
Intertwine their
Gold and silver
Souls in ecstasy.
O hear ye, see
Them blazing praise
To the glory
Of the realm to come
And Giovanni Gabrielli.

MOZART

Who like you knew genius is to serve?—
Who gave us music in the which
We learn to get over our crankiness,
To work our souls to make ourselves
Graceful and gay that life may be
Allegro for those around us,
Be they no more than Franz Josephs?

A LOOK AROUND

It's a miracle most people know
How to look and where to go.
Have they seen some revelation
I have missed? I question.

A PRESENTIMENT

Is it credible
That all these people
Swinging livers in the street,
With a passing generation
Shall have met one destination
Underneath the whirling feet?

SICILIAN NOCTURNE (NOTTURNO SICILIANO)

When the glare of day has at last seeped away
And the air ceased to sweat, crackle, and fret,
And dropping its perfumes, dewy, wet,
An evening gown has been wrapped around
The harbor where late the sun set;

When the town has at last settled down,
Its market riot and traffic vibration
Drowned out by the rhythmical surge of the ocean,
Whose eventide waves the isle lave
Washing its burnt feet in aqueous lotion;

Then comes the hour, the accession of power,
When distracted from daydream I mount the stair,
And from rooftop into the misting air
Pour a sojourner's will, regret, tears, and desire
To cultivate all that is strange and fair.

For the night sparkles around me, the stars on the sea,
And the city glimmers astonishingly,
And I know that in this far-flung reach of the earth
For me, a transient, there is infinite, ungraspable worth
And just too much beauty, O Sicily, O Italy!

Palermo Skyline

SICILIAN FRIEND

Hair bleached sandy by the sun,
Eyes diffusing light upon
Olive-oiled skin so tender
I think there must be vision there,
My sensational sweet Sicilian.

Mondello, Sicily

PASQUA, MONDELLO (SICILY)

The sea is breathing warm and sweet,
The sands are piled white and high,
About the mountains' chalky feet
The seagulls scream their cry.

Heat pervading through the sky
In waves is shaken from the sun,
Which tinctures in an ochre blaze
Earth, atmosphere, and ocean.

Now commence the scented days
When wakened bodies walk abroad.
Sound and color multiply,
New dresses seek the promenade.

And one who'd forgotten and quite disbelieved
That sensual life can be satisfying
Is now most gratefully relieved
For some respite from dying.

TO HIS FORMER MISTRESS

World enough and time there be
For those whose patience lets them see
How things together stand. And lady,

If I understand your position now
Indeed it's finally clear to me how
You have felt all along. You know,

I only wanted you to prove
That you did not want me to shove:
So no more will you hear me talk of love.

Rather will I follow you
Uniting myself also to
The ungifted and foul. For it's true

That essential goods in humanity
Are just those we share equally,
Or at least should. And insofar as morally

The better are precisely those
Who hold themselves as nearly close
To all the rest, I'll nothing more impose.

I accept your wanting to be alone
Or rather to be with everyone
So you can grow. What's more, I own

That pursuing only people who
Have something coveted by you
Is no right way to live. I knew

That only loving all at once
Could one love any a genuine ounce
And further needed only this comeuppance.

And though but briefly our days flicker
Surely they will not vanish quicker
For our present understanding. Only thicker

Suffused in undeflected light revealing
The passion with which all creation always is appealing
Our time opens into an undated universe of feeling.

FOR GRACE AND COMPANY

I sat upon the shore and heard
The children laughing in the sea.
Let them laugh, I gravely said,
They have not such deep thoughts as me.

I stood upon the shore and watched them
Loving play and playfully loving:
What beautiful vanity, I thought,
It's a shame it comes to nothing.

I lay upon my strand and sensed
Their dolphining within the waves
And in a plight wished human life
Were free for what it craves.

O wisdom, traitor, who tell all but nothing give,
Let me be foolish and wrong but let me live.
Maturity, murderer of every infant wish,
The teeth you use come from a plastic dish.
Virtue, off with your fine gold net,
Through which nothing whole passes: let me get wet.

Better the giddy, undignified flights
On spread wings tilting for heaven
Free from conceit of restraint, where the leaven
Of creaturely pleasures and praises unites
In simplicity sisters and brothers.

A ball was bouncing on the ocean:
"Sport with me," it seemed to say,
"Come get wet and waste your motion,
It's good only for today."

I shall dash into the sea and take the surf upon my breast,
Fling my limbs into a chaos, lose my breath.
How can I know that the long run be futile?
Nay, I'll believe it may be fully blest,
And at least it will be actual.

TO THE UNKNOWN STRANGER

(*L'Étranger* of Albert Camus)

O Stranger, lover of the world that is,
Oblivious to what it's meant to be
By those who make up meanings:
You wished to be with humanity
On the day your head rolled for the French,
With them to the end,
Though the bond be hatred.
You are human, that's what's plain to see
In a world where everything else is dodgy.
In a sense I'd fain take off my head to you.

TAIZÉ

Taizé, place of worship
And encounters of so many with the Lord
And one another, young folk searching:
Yet still a little village
In the immemorial of rural France,
Stone croppings up the hillside
Round the kirk and its cemetery:
O tiny immeasurable site,
Pinpoint bearing on the map of eternity,
How can you loom so large to me?
I walked along your ridge road
When the sun suffused the sky
With a glorious warm vermillion
Bleeding down to your sensitive valley.
Your earth shone rosily on the road
And reflected from rooftops into air
Which tinkled with the soft flock's foraging.
O Taizé, I walked through you
For the only time for ever,
And yet walking with me there
I sensed my whole heart's history.
What do your mountains mean?

What hides behind your skies?
Why do I feel that my lifetime
Is not enough for your liturgy?

MYTH AND ELOPEMENT

To Cinzia (first met at Taizé)

Bridges arise on all sides
In connections many and diverse.
We're dead center of a civilization
At the confluence of its rivers.

You stretch your arms to me,
A majestic gesture, youthful goddess:
You have embraced infinity
With your hardiness.

The bridges of Paris on their knees
Bow down before what we have shared:
Grander than all this work of centuries
What your eighteen years have dared.

FARING WELL IN ARMS

(Thanks, Ernest, for the stylistic tip)

A little girl
whose body bulges
in the right places
drives me mad.
The way she sits
is a magnet
that draws me
implacably
hard as iron
fast to her hips.
It's the way it
fits together, you know,
the soul, that makes
each part so
irresistibly delicious
to stick to.
Her face is sweet
when I see it
all that's girl is
expressed in its

features good to eat
with no sugar frosting
or makeup on.
Her kisses suck
so deep and she hugs
so tight that I die
just to start to love her.
And after I lie
with my arms
round a person
I only begin to know
who I want alone
as my lover.

YOU ARE WOMAN

You are woman, I see
In your fruit-shaped thumbs
In your skin licked smooth
With foreign gums.
You sail strange hemispheres
Into my sea
Catching my wind away.

CARPE DIEM

Soles occidere et redire possunt
nobis cum semel occidit brevis lux,
nox est perpetua una dormienda

—Catullus (84–54 BC)

(Suns can set and rise again
But once our brief light's set
It's one perpetual night of sleep)

Every living vibration thumps dead inside me.
Marilyn washing the dishes, Tammy playing,
The model train going round on its track—
All are cries of extinction
Going to maximum distension
Entropic annihilation
And no one to ever mind that they've gone on.

On a beach, a girl
In a bathing suit, walking,
She could be in love with you.

The sun, the sand
Press you warmly to follow.
Your flesh is in motion.

There's no war now.
Your life's yours,
Catch what you can from it.

The day blazing
Now is high, later tumbles
Over the edge of the world.
O pursue it!

FREE RIDING

I

Roads of France and Italy
Engines singing
Lorry drivers suffering miles along.
A package of Gitanes discarded
Girates to its roadside destination
To disintegrate. The miles weep.
From beforehand they're consumed
Steady and pitiless
Devoured under the ravenous hood.
Behind the wastes are spewed
Into vanishing distances.

II

Silken pine steep
Alpine flowing early
Morning dampness sets
In dark of night the height
Perpetually cool and wet
And murmuring all things sweet

(while a lorry driver takes a leak)
all things the night
purifying in inaccessible
mountain fastnesses.

III

Illuminated valley
Spread below the
Balcony at night
Like a pin cushion
Pine-soft light-pricked.
The voyagers ploughing
Through fog soft
Headlights forward
Breaking the unknown
Only road.

LIGHT MUSIC

The hills of France roll on
and on and on
and on their flowing slopes
plays the sun
musically in the wheat
a grainy harmony
in varied barley.
I hear the song
of the wind
accompanied by
the wind.

LIGHT

Light
Lying in the valley
Like a golden skein
Of immortal fleece, like the glory
Of Israel's prophets and their sublime,
Strikes
Right on the corner
And materializes church-brick existence,
Spirit incarnate in
Infinite concrete perfectness
Called to be by
Light.

Transitional
(Between Lands and Mindsets)

DANCE OF THE SHIRTS

The dance of the shirts on the laundry line
Across the back alley when they're not being worn,
When the inside of life is out and outside's spread
Out wide in space and the light of day.
Utterly unaffected they hang
In their scene and century with the walls,
After the work and worry
After the compromise and the muddling through.
Clean and light, sprightly they dance
In the joy of existence merely, behind all facades,
Where the sun still comes,
Unnoticed, knowing all.

OUTSIGHT

Sometimes in the honesty which
unsuccess brings I am left
with feeling truth is lingering
unseen disguised as innocence
behind light-blue shadowed lids.

Mirrored in the clouds I see myself
swimming out alone in the ocean
nude speck on the great earth's
eyeball mucous, luxuriously stuck
in heroic poses. And all wet.

O unmask me, pitiless peering
tokens of beauty born to be
with your preference life and death
conferring, which makes you laugh,
creating and destroying unwittingly.

HUMAN COIN

Bars and restaurants loud with people
Dressed up trying to live a little
Before it's too late.
The conference table, dark and dense,
Reflects the bitter countenance
Of bargainers with fate.
By its severe, its antic face,
Who would suspect the human case,
So dear, so delicate?

UNIVERSE OF POSSIBILITIES?

Every hour of every day
Our few light years roll away.
Eyeballs fixed in photographs
Glimmer of a star collapsed.
People in their constellations
Mutate into new relations.
Of all possible universes
There's none but the one that is.

UNCHARITABLE ANTI-CLERICAL POEM

Jacques was a dandy boy and fine
Christian, though he'd have rather been
A swine.
Renunciation became for him the royal way:
He never got the candy.
Always someone else got that
Which Jacques was so desirous of,
Until privation itself turned to meat
And the bishop blessed it.
A feast prepared in the desert:
For God's sake,
What miraculous compensations people make.

A SCENT OF SEX IN THE SUMMERTIME

A scent of sex in the summertime
Around the pool's edge: sun-decked
Arms and legs, breasts, bellies
Laid out wide for the sun's rich kiss.

A cult of bodies, beautiful
In the open day disgusts not,
Rather fills the soul with longing
For the beauty that will not peal.

O Lord, I long for your bright pavilions
hovering in the air
of inspiration, dewed with the sweetness
constant caring gives.

Raise me up in body
to be with you where you are,
to behold the beauty of the Lord
Everlastingly!

ORIGINAL LYRIC

Lyrical green and yellow
enamel the meadow
in light made syrup-like
by remembrance
of singings past.
Notes a mother sang
blithe in the garden
sunlight long ago
pass through pages
of cortex
theology wrapped
round the inner ear.
Over voluble sages
the earliest lyric
ecstatically comes back home
to the illuminated ear
where it was born.

KNOWLEDGE

Without protoplasmic touch
Can the mind encompass much?
Roll the world into a ball
With one word—“universal”—
Yes, but all the thought within the head
All the visions on the bed
Can’t forestall that, come one day
The hour when slant light drops away
Down from the study you emerge
Upon a pitch-black forest’s verge.

LETTER TO A FRIEND IN COLOR

Dear Larry
Hi there!
I'm on the West-bound speeding home
With my eyes shut seeing green
And I think of you.

Changing to purple now
And violet like the sea
That's how they change, my emotions.

I think of you off in Paris
In a pastel
Of delicious mists!

I'm glad you are doing it
Someone must
To relieve the dull hopeless
Work we all do in this city

Feeling blue
I think of you
(past dread rows of ash can dwellings)
up to your ears in mauve!

LIMBO

A faint dull pallor
on cement blocks and parking lot
serves notice of return of day.
Excited disembodied babble
All about the world somewhere
Is on the air.
In an enlightened cabinet
Someone's de-naturing his face,
Says a dribbling water faucet,
To go upon the shift and take his place.
I can't get up
I have not slept, I have not loved
and except for all that's led me here—
left me lying flat as if forever—
I've nothing to do.
Today should I plan something new?
Yet I would, I would, again, yet again
Anything at all, if only I knew.

AT SEA

Rudder cutting through the ocean
Sail dividing wide the sky
Misty line on the horizon—
So traveling I am not I.

Ebbs and flows the deep main swelling
Up against the atmosphere
In constant strife, but there's no telling
Whether you are here or there.

Of idealisms I'd thought better
Lowered down the clean-cut flag,
Sank my feet into the water
Back of stern to drag.

Now different tacks are all so equal
That it's hard to follow one
Instead of going round in a circle
Noting where each comes undone.

Was I wrong from the beginning
Or did somewhere lose the way,
Or's the trip just this sort of thing
Leading me to port some day?

Britannic
(Oxford and London)

THE PIETY OF THINKING

It's like catching the wind
One must wait and hope
And when it comes you sail free.
It's like catching the wind—
Impossible. It catches you from behind
And lifts you from your knee.

*

O holy tree
The veil of thy divinity
I fear to rend,
Across the scraps of abstract thought to send
beauty revealed to me.

*

Lord, thy universe is puzzling;
Nothing equals reality—
Infinitely gentle, infinitely suffering,
More sublime than morality.

*

The philosopher labors day by day
Trying to invent reality.
The washerwoman plies her board
In weariness of the chore.

O vision radiant white,
Clothed in beams of light,
Lift their faces to thy glory
Scatter blessings on their heads,
Kiss her hands and stroke his neck
Solace them with thine own story.

IN ENGLISH MEADOW

In English meadow I sit and read
The testaments of Eternity.
The undulating ages breed
In waves of thought around me.

*

Mid flowers fair and adorable
In contemplations peaceable
Lo, Faith softly hymning her canticles
And the trees rustling with oracles.

DIVINITY LIBRARY

Where are they now, all the inward hours
With the divinity library's lamplight spent
Wrestling with principalities and powers
Pensively, pendulously bent?
I gaze at the old gothic cupola
And it looks just the same.
Discernible is not the least *differentia*
Which from those mental strivings came.
Yet inwardly edified, invisibly shorn
A heart is transformed, a new life is born.
Even without knowing against whom
Or how or for what I fought,
By my faith I now am
What then I was taught.

(Radcliffe Camera, Bodleian Libraries, University of Oxford)

Figure 8. Radcliffe Camera, Bodleian Libraries, University of Oxford

REASONING IS NOT WHAT IT PURPORTS TO BE

Reasoning is not what it purports to be.
It is no tight-linked chain of necessity.
It no more than suggests a possibility
Of how someone might think and see.
It is a plausible or pleasing hypothesis
And not something that really is.

IMITATION OF CAMPION

Dance thou smoothly
In measures mete,
Move thou lithely
With rhythmic feet,
Sing thou tunely
In melodies sweet,
Sound thou finely
With notes discrete.
As thou art pretty
My lovely Ditty
May all combine along
In perfect song.

SHAKESPEARE IN THE PARK

You move me, bright actress
With gently flaming motion,
Through night air on my soul impress
Your every sweetest notion.

JENNY ARRANGING HERSELF TO PLAY VIOLIN: AN APPRECIATION BY HER PIANIST

A perfect fitness in the clothes
Every delicate feature shows
Of that fair frame.
And the same
By harmony in every part
Makes a symphony within my heart:
So that when any limb moves,
As by conductor's art
My heart loves.

LIGHTSPOT

your knee bends
your calf is
quite unconscious
of itself
like a willow
bending
softly aglow
by the crescent moon

euclidean
primary shape
in a luminous skin
the heavenly sphere
reflecting
fully in sight
of night's dark longing

GLIMPSES

I

Not a person
That's too focused
Too officious
Overbearing.
Just the angle
Of a skirt where
It flares from the
Leg so tender.

II

Woman wrapped in
Fur and linen
Stands regarding
Window scene,
By the ashlar
Rows behind her
Neatly closed in
An expression.

III

Women I have known on buses
Theatres, passing in the street,
Give off scents of something just as
Intimate as being your Mrs.
And more maddeningly sweet.

THE WATER TOWER

Every night I look out of my window
And see the water tower,
Its beady little red lights
Always steady, always staring.
And I imagine my own helpless
Wriggling sinews doubled
Round one of its iron girdings,
Drooping downward.
The blind grey tower
Rips the sky
Complexioned soft and yellow
In the haze at sunset
Or cerulean blue at night.
Yet of all the fragile hues and textures
That bold rection punctures
It never fathoms one.
I fathom those skies,
I fathom the tower too:
It can nail its iron into me
Cross me with hard bars
Seal me in a system watertight.
But still this heeding sense is mine

And in it I am infinite:
So long as I can suffer
I'll see a sky with color
And shall not be dismantled of my glory.

THE AUTOMOCRAT

I sit here in the upper flights
Of my twentieth-century furnished flat.
The building functions day and night,
Humming like a laundromat.
Aircraft glide across the window,
Traffic circulates below,
And I suspended in the midst
Seem not to exist.
(I am here only invisibly
Hidden in virtual reality.)
From here I know about everything—
Space and Egyptology and news—
For all this the media bring
Or just the *Sunday Times* reviews.
I switch the television on and see
All round the planet
Life's inexhaustible pageantry
As well as horrors like to can it.[1]
Charles at his cricket club,
Arabs on some terrorist job:

1. In some London dialects, "like" is used to mean "likely," and "to can" something is to unceremoniously put an end to it. "Can it" is often used to mean simply "shut up."

Both look alike to me:
Pretty colors on TV.

PASSING THE NATIONAL GALLERY, TRAFALGAR SQUARE

A parasol twirling in the rain
Paisley colors
Seen from the upper deck of a bus
Spreads and then flutters.
What sweet relief
From drab concrete
This little unplanned exhibition:
Through ripply-waved
Glass rain-glazed
It paints an impression.

Figure 9. Trafalgar Square and National Gallery, London

ON *WORK* BY FORD MADDOX BROWN

Around the seasoned girth of those arms
Revolves the universe; placed in perspective,
Fixed in social history as in paint
The worker works; his serene forehead
Cocked back on its axis of the earth,
Monumental against the ground
Of colorful evanescent social classes.

Figure 10. *Work*, by Ford Maddox Brown, Manchester Art Gallery

THE STREET ENTERTAINERS, COVENT GARDEN

They come miming and rhyming, juggling and struggling to escape,
The magical, comic, mad, musical street entertainers.
With no theatres to bill them
No proscenium
They leap into the street
And perform on concrete,
Their only retainers
Being motley and their own audacity:
Throwbacks to a stage where time is still real,
Not a dream of the past in a sleep after dinner
Nor anticipations of a fantastic future,
But a tightrope wire that cuts sheer through flesh
In a split second's violence.
It's the time of judgment in which they live,
Of the rude laugh and heckle
Or the ecstatic sparkle
Of a right trick, success, stardom, beauty spontaneous free!
Not guardedly eked out by prestige and publicity.
There's one in particular,
A most peerless juggler
Who by tricks and trifles, gambits, and ham

Makes mockery of his own talent.
Half-naked, prostrating
His quips and cracks begging
Indulgence, he gives himself for our enjoyment,
To us, not to art, he makes his plea
With no high invulnerable dignity,
Just the immediate truth
Of the pudding's proof.
And then when the act ends
Dear ladies and gents
And he holds out his cupped hands
For five or ten pence,
How gently tempered, how clement he waits,
Having just swallowed fire,
While the circumspect crowd hesitates.
Yet of all the examples,
Iconic idols and models
Of success in this fine society,
It is you that I emulate
You that communicate
Straight, and spark on the bare blade of life
Where pride and person are clean exposed
And the senses race keen.
And when at day's darkening
You gather your coinbox
Your plumes and your props,
It is you who I wish
To think tenderly loved,
You who have passed through

The great tribulation and purged
Like gold in a refiner's fire
Your nobly sensitive soul.

Figure 11. Covent Garden, London

GREEN PARK, LONDON

Green Park, in the spring,
Its first white blossoms showering
From the trees in the breeze: they angle down
To the smooth velvet underlying lawn,
And drawn like a spread pulled back they disclose
A figure fluttering with the wind in her clothes.

I am sure that I do not nor ever have known her,
And yet that carriage, that step, that demeanor—
I think all might be
That of one I knew intimately.

Has she changed? I wonder
And does she still dream
And does she remember
Things that have been?

For perhaps she meanders
In parks all alone
And at such times remembers
What we two have known.

She has changed, I am sure
And yet don't know how
Or which feelings endure
Or what ways she may grow.

The figure has turned now and flickers from sight,
The blossoms thick covering green beneath white,
And all I wanted was a glimpse of her face,
To know what remembrance my memory may chase.

Figure 12. Green Park, London

CYRENIAN[2] SENTIMENTS

Healthy, smiling people adorn the streets.
Should I envy the couples going arm in arm?
Do they crush their mouths together that way,
Ostentatiously, thinking they tantalize me?
There's a dog in the alley from whose opening I spy.
He is poking his muzzle through garbage bags.
Chewing he looks up at me, winces, and then wags:
We are in sympathy.

2. Named after Simon of Cyrene, who according to the Gospels (Matthew 27:32; Mark 15:21; and Luke 23:26) helped Jesus carry his cross to Calvary, the Cyrenians provide housing and support to single, homeless people with dire handicaps and special needs in London. A term of service with them produced this poem, among others.

ST. PATRICK'S DAY DANCE

St. Patrick's Day dance,
Bless his holy bones
With the blessing of rotating flesh—
Makes the sign of the cross—
And excited blood.
It sprinkles the legs, necks, arms, faces
With crimson, and mingles—
What heads dizzied scarcely admit—
The orgy of bacchanalian rites
With color of sacrifice.
Yet now, very now, is the agony there
As heels fly up kicking high into the air,
And all come to the point of explosion within
And that's where the music stops.
Music takes you so far
And then precepts of life
If you want to be like
Old Saint Patrick take over.
Thus obedient sons and daughters fair
May be venerable bones beneath clover.

CHRISTIAN LOVE

The congregation divagates
Down shadowed streets of private life.
A thousand souls' experiences
Each separate, yet alike
Stream in thousand rivulets
From the Fountain of all light.
Did you feel we were together
In the Kyrié Eléison
As if by no ungentle quaver
Could our union be undone?
Yet my confession is ever
How I long to follow someone.
47 Eastgate Street
Heels click up steps
Nice stockinged calves
Door clapped shut—retreat.
What do I want? I contemplate
The beauty of each person
And wish each in the Lord complete.
It's just I think I love someone.

O GOD

God, show me what is beautiful
Now and forever.
Flesh, I know, will only wither,
Knowledge harden to conceit,
Innocence is culpable
In a world of gross deceit.
God, is there anything I can do
That will be beautiful to you?

DOVES ARE DWELLING

Doves are dwelling all along the spiritual flyway,
The cornices of every story house them.
I know not whither the rise ascends,
You can cling to either tilt of the roof
And climb to no summit.

*

On clamorous wings the white doves climb
The conic vault of tessellated time.

*

Waves of history, thought, strife, love
Reverberating complexity
Upon the sea of modernity
And smoothly gliding over all—the Dove.

O THAT MY PRAYER

O that my prayer be pleasing
To him who enhances
By joy without ceasing
My moonlight trances.

THE CONTEMPLATIVE'S EYES

The contemplative's eyes
Opened like a sunrise.

O for that mystical love
More sublime than emotion,
Finer than any graspable notion,
Rising to heavenly things above
Through the soul's humbly bowing
Beneath a cloud of unknowing.

Pitiable and adorable, aren't we?
Fretting away our eternal hours,
O you saints who laugh to see,
Winking from the stars.

Reminiscence and Contemporaneity

CONTEMPORARIES

She was never my wife;
I'd not even have called her my girlfriend.
As the relationship now appears to me
She was simply my contemporary.
Better so, so exquisitely intimate
To be both in the flesh
Together at one time on one planet.
She was here at this college when I was.
She was fresh, sweet, and aspiring when I was,
Physically present together in roundness of limb.
To think even this courtyard we daily crossed
Each of us, sometimes simultaneously
Crossing one side to the other.
We lived much in the mind in those days
But never, almost, thought ourselves lonely.
We lived with the blessed immortal ones.
Yet never, I think, did we realize
Between Plato and eighteenth-century Paris
And Jesus Christ
What it meant or might mean
To be together at one time in one place,
To be meant for each other
As contemporaries.

RECOLLECTION

In the parlor sounds a wistful tune
From under the slant lid of a grand piano
And winds among the lacquered furnishings
Laced with violet shades of afternoon.

The weave is patterned with a distant dream
Of other lands and former centuries.
Yet here at home in the deep south and summer
In the solo piano's clear liquid whine
Under the unfaded sun's yellow enamel
I think sits all of history reclined:

Stretched from one end of the earth
To the other, quiet contemplation surveys
All that the world's madness purveys
And ponders life's inestimable worth.

MAY 15

The middle day of May
Upon me
Rubbed into my skin
Breathed in.
The winter's past,
The year is far advanced
Before I know it
Or am set.
What if age itself should thus surprise
By striking
Quicker than the eye
That has been drowsing?

MARCH

Where's that breath coming from?
March I've known before
licks in through the window cracked.
From roots within me
spring juices of juvenescence
not yet missed.
I'll sing this season,
books behind me closed,
I know enough now.
Now I'll go
with the breeze in feeling
freshly my way over the fair show.

MEDITATION ON A BUS

Let me live always within that transition
as when waiting on a bus at night
being delayed by insouciance
of public servants killing time

with a sudden sharp shock the bands pop
of frustration tightening
round vitals within

and all of a sudden something's overcome
somewhere a battle is lost and won
renunciation is ended and begun

And the one-time bus ride I'm on registers:
finally, I am
in the land of the living
amidst jostling limbs
my limbs might jostle with
their movements moving me
as if answering to their volitions.

Now this sympathetic confluence sends me
longingly back in memory to when
schoolmates tagged me.
Our lives undistinguished then
Were brutally bound in common.
I remember the bad and the beautiful
all rolled together in play on the ground.
I remember I wondered what would
in the end become of us all:
by God, at least then we were tangible.

What's more rewarding
than being aged, than possessing
a history personal to oneself alone?
Like reclaiming from an artificial lake
islands one recognizes one has lived on
as they spread into an archipelago!

SOMETHING TO TELL YOU

tonight I am tumbling
out of mind
through my body
steep inside me
past all catches
where distinctions
keep their fine nets
torn by your beauty
deep inside me
bearing down
to the bottom well
re-echoing sound
fraught with loveliness
thought can't think
and astonished
by unmediated
life alive
in you, in me

THIS LIFE

Then let me face my death
Today
If it's the final truth
I want
To live in it and not within illusions.
These veins
The messiness of flesh
And squeamish
Plastic mold of face
Are all I've got to live on, I admit it.
Now let me press them into shape
And make
Their flimsiness serve until
Some definite contribution take
Its form in history—
Then dissolve.

AN ACCIDENT

Tonight I am mourning an accident
That in fact never happened
Because it's an accident that it did not happen.
And therefore I tremble and make lamentation
And prostrate myself in contrition of heart
For the unforgiveable carelessness
Which is yet forgiven, and I go free
And the world's unscathed
By what could have,
Really even should have happened
But for an accident unforeseen
And unforeseeable by me.
There's nothing to see now,
There's no time or place
With a trace
Of the times and places missed—
The dreary roadside wreckage,
Blood in the ambulance,
Names and dates in stone—
Because time and place
Failed fractionally
To coincide with one another

And sped clean past
On their unreflecting trajectories forever.
But can it really have made no difference?
Is everything possibly different,
Possibly nothing,
And I'm the same?
Is there nothing at all,
No inference?
I stand gaping appalled
Before the abyss with shame.

UNAWARES

Between the rays of the sun
that illumine the visible
objectivity of things

Between the time frames
that schedules of transport
school and job arrange

Between the downtown place
and the home and recreation place
between room and room

a process continually is
transpiring, a life
decisively is being lived

in the hidden reaches
beyond mind's control
within the soul

a poem is being composed
an unseen vision being envisioned
in sensitive veins

a dormant prophet is
becoming indignant
about to break out

a martyr carefully, cautiously
prepares a sacrifice
he does not yet accept

most of all a child in spite
of himself is being loved
into loving

APPENDIX:
SUPPLEMENTARY PHOTO ALBUM

Figure 13. Turin Skyline from Monte dei Cappuccini

Figure 14. Turin: Piazza Vittorio and the Mole Antonelliana, Alps Aerial Overview

Figure 15. Venice, Grand Canal

Figure 16. Canals of Venice

Figure 17. Grand Canal, Venice, with Rialto Bridge

Figure 18. Politeama Garibaldi, Palermo

Figure 19. Covent Garden, London, Street Entertainers

Figure 20. Radcliffe Camera, Bodleian Libraries, University of Oxford

Figure 21. Radcliffe Camera interior (History Library and Humanities Reading Room)

Figure 22. Pusey House Divinity Library, Oxford

Figure 23. National Gallery, Trafalgar Square

Figure 24. Green Park

www.ingramcontent.com/pod-product-compliance
Lightning Source LLC
LaVergne TN
LVHW090528110826
845146LV00003B/1018

9798385264766